PRAYERS

WRITTEN·AT· VAILIMA·BY· ROBERT·LOUIS· STEVENSON·

THE·INTRODUC=
TION·BY·MRS·R·
·L·STEVENSON

IN every Samoan household the day is closed with prayer and the sing= ing of hymns. The omission of this sacred duty would indicate, not only a lack of religious training in the house chief, but a shameless disregard of all that is reputable in Samoan social life. No doubt, to many, the evening service is no more than a duty fulfilled. The child who says his prayer at his mother's knee can have no real conception of the meaning of the words he lisps so readily, yet he goes to his little bed with a sense of heavenly protection that he would miss were the prayer forgotten. The average Samoan is but a larger child in most things, and would lay an uneasy head on his wooden pillow if he had not joined, even perfunc= torily, in the evening service.

With my husband, prayer, the direct appeal, was a necessity. When he was happy he felt impelled to offer thanks for that undeserved joy; when in sorrow, or pain, to call for strength to bear what must be borne.

VAILIMA lay up some three miles of continual rise from Apia, and more than half that distance from the nearest village. It was a long way for a tired man to walk down every evening with the sole purpose of joining in family worship; and the road through the bush was dark, and, to the Samoan imagination, beset with supernatural terrors. Wherefore, as soon as our household had fallen into a regular routine, and the bonds of Samoan family life began to draw us more closely together, Tusitala felt the necessity of including our retainers in our evening devotions. I suppose ours was the only white man's family in all Samoa, except those of the missionaries, where the day naturally ended with this homely, patriarchal custom. Not only were the religious scruples of the natives satisfied, but, what we did not foresee, our own respectability — and incidentally that of our retainers — became assured, and the influence of Tusitala increased tenfold.

After all work and meals were finished, the 'pu,' or war conch, was sounded from the back veranda and the front, so that it might be heard by all. I don't think it ever occurred to us that there was any incongruity in the use of the war conch for the peaceful invitation to prayer. In response to its summons the white members of the family took their usual places in one end of the large hall, while the Samoans — men, women, and children — trooped in through all the open doors, some carrying lanterns if the evening were dark, all moving quietly and dropping with Samoan decorum in a wide semicircle on the floor beneath a great lamp that hung from the ceiling. The service began by my son reading a chapter from the Samoan Bible, Tusitala following with a prayer in English, some times impromptu, but more often from the notes in this little book, interpolating or changing with the circumstances of the day. Then came the singing of one or more hymns in the native tongue, and the recitation in concert of the Lord's Prayer, also in Samoan. Many of these hymns were set to ancient tunes, very wild and warlike, and strangely at variance with the missionary words.

Sometimes a passing band of hostile warriors, with blackened faces, would peer in at us through the open windows, and often we were forced to pause until the strangely savage, monotonous noise of the native drums had ceased; but no Samoan, nor, I trust, white person, changed his reverent attitude. Once, I remember a look of surprised dismay crossing the countenance of Tusitala when my son, contrary to his usual custom of reading the next chapter following that of yesterday, turned back the leaves of his Bible to find a chapter fiercely denunciatory,

and only too applicable to the foreign dic-
tators of distracted Samoa. On another
occasion the chief himself brought the
service to a sudden check. He had just
learned of the treacherous conduct of one
in whom he had every reason to trust.
That evening the prayer seemed unusual-
ly short and formal. As the singing
stopped he arose abruptly and left the
room. I hastened after him, fearing some
sudden illness. 'What is it?' I asked.
'It is this,' was the reply; I am not yet fit
to say, "Forgive us our trespasses as we
forgive those who trespass against us." '

It is with natural reluctance that I
touch upon the last prayer of my husband's
life. Many have supposed that he
showed, in the wording of this prayer,
that he had some premonition of his
approaching death. I am sure he had no
such premonition. It was I who told the
assembled family that I felt an impending
disaster approaching nearer and nearer.
Any Scot will understand that my state-
ment was received seriously. It could not

be, we thought, that danger threatened any
one within the house; but Mr. Graham Bal
four, my husband's cousin, very near and
dear to us, was away on a perilous cruise.
Our fears followed the various vessels, &
more or less unseaworthy, in which he was
making his way from island to island to
the atoll where the exiled king, Mataafa,
was at that time imprisoned. In my husband's
last prayer, the night before his death, he
asked that we should be given strength to
bear the loss of this dear friend, should such
a sorrow befall us.

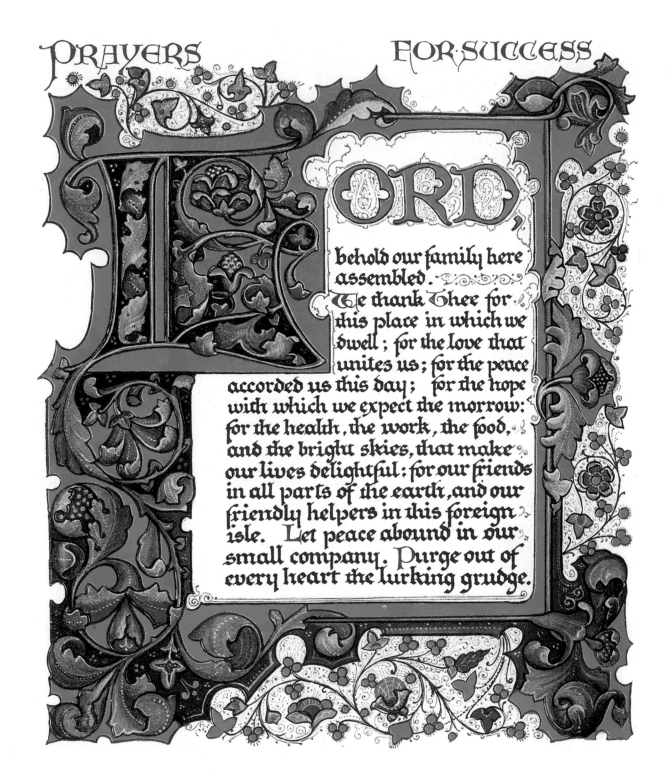

LORD, behold our family here assembled. We thank Thee for this place in which we dwell; for the love that unites us; for the peace accorded us this day; for the hope with which we expect the morrow: for the health, the work, the food, and the bright skies, that make our lives delightful: for our friends in all parts of the earth, and our friendly helpers in this foreign isle. Let peace abound in our small company. Purge out of every heart the lurking grudge.

Give us grace and strength to forbear and to persevere. Offenders, give us the grace to accept and to forgive offenders. Forgetful ourselves, help us to bear cheerfully the forgetfulness of others. Give us courage and gaiety and the quiet mind. Spare to us our friends, soften to us our enemies. Bless us, if it may be, in all our innocent endeavours. If it may not, give us the strength to encounter that which is to come, that we be brave in peril, constant in tribulation, temperate in wrath, and in all changes of fortune, and, down to the gates of death, loyal and loving one to another. As the clay to the potter, as the wind mill to the wind, as children of their sire, we beseech of Thee this help and mercy for Christ's sake:

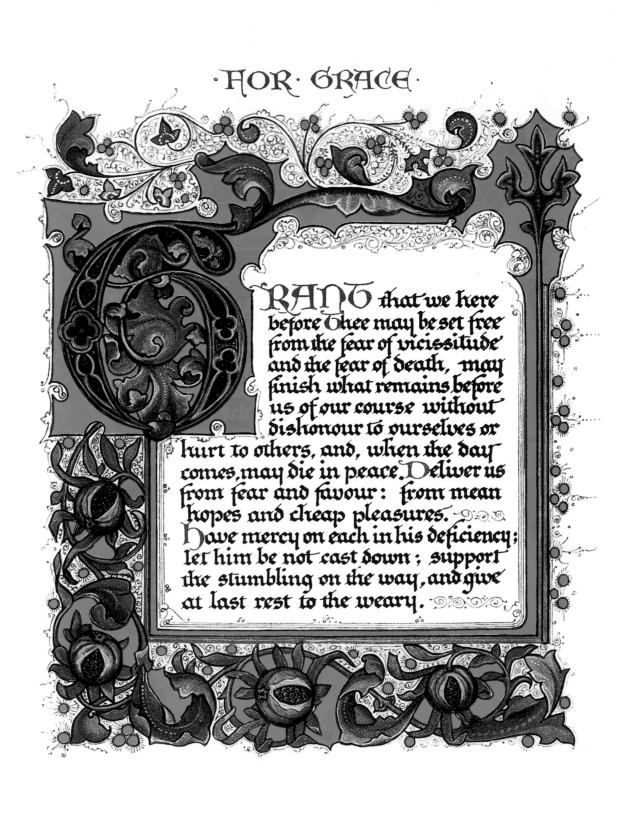

GRANT that we here before Thee may be set free from the fear of vicissitude and the fear of death, may finish what remains before us of our course without dishonour to ourselves or hurt to others, and, when the day comes, may die in peace. Deliver us from fear and favour: from mean hopes and cheap pleasures. Have mercy on each in his deficiency; let him be not cast down; support the stumbling on the way, and give at last rest to the weary.

The day returns and brings us the petty round of irritating concerns and duties. Help us to play the man, help us to perform them with laughter and kind faces, let cheerfulness abound with industry. Give us to go blithely on our business all this day, bring us to our resting beds weary and content and undishonoured, and grant us in the end the gift of sleep.

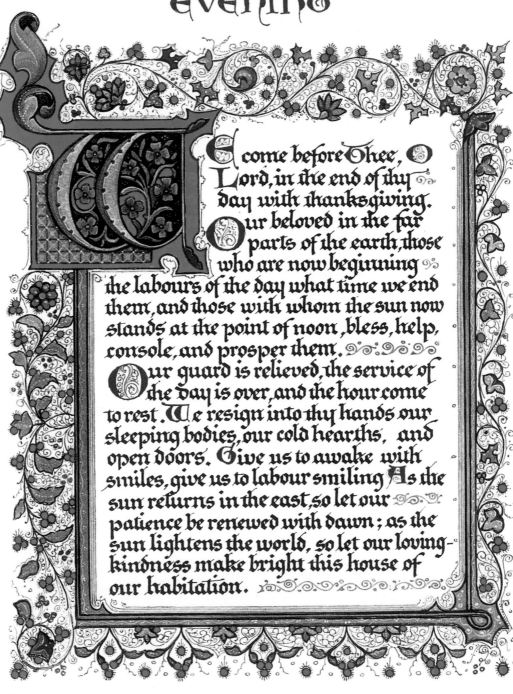

WE come before Thee, O Lord, in the end of thy day with thanksgiving. Our beloved in the far parts of the earth, those who are now beginning the labours of the day what time we end them, and those with whom the sun now stands at the point of noon, bless, help, console, and prosper them.

Our guard is relieved, the service of the day is over, and the hour come to rest. We resign into thy hands our sleeping bodies, our cold hearths, and open doors. Give us to awake with smiles, give us to labour smiling As the sun returns in the east, so let our patience be renewed with dawn; as the sun lightens the world, so let our loving-kindness make bright this house of our habitation.

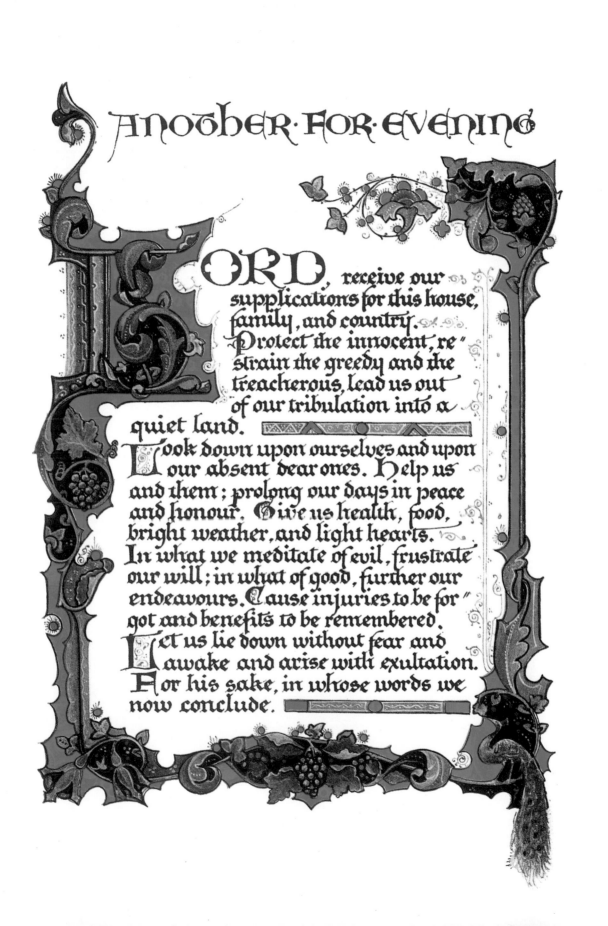

LORD, receive our supplications for this house, family, and country. Protect the innocent, restrain the greedy and the treacherous, lead us out of our tribulation into a quiet land.

Look down upon ourselves and upon our absent dear ones. Help us and them; prolong our days in peace and honour. Give us health, food, bright weather, and light hearts. In what we meditate of evil, frustrate our will; in what of good, further our endeavours. Cause injuries to be forgot and benefits to be remembered.

Let us lie down without fear and awake and arise with exultation. For his sake, in whose words we now conclude.

WE thank Thee, Lord, for the glory of the late days and the excellent face of thy sun. We thank Thee for good news received. We thank Thee for the pleasures we have enjoyed and for those we have been able to confer. And now, when the clouds gather and the rain impends over the forest and our house, permit us not to be cast down; let us not lose the savour of past mercies and past pleasures; but, like the voice of a bird singing in the rain, let grateful memory survive in the hour of darkness. If there be in front of us any painful duty, strengthen us with the grace of courage; if any act of mercy, teach us tenderness and patience.

LORD,

Thou sendest down rain upon the uncounted millions of the forest, and givest the trees to drink exceedingly. We are here upon this isle a few handfuls of men, and how many myriads upon myriads of stalwart trees! Teach us the lesson of the trees. The sea around us, which this rain recruits, teems with the race of fish; teach us Lord, the meaning of the fishes. Let us see ourselves for what we are, one out of the countless number of the clans of thy handiwork. When we would despair, let us remember that these also please and serve Thee.

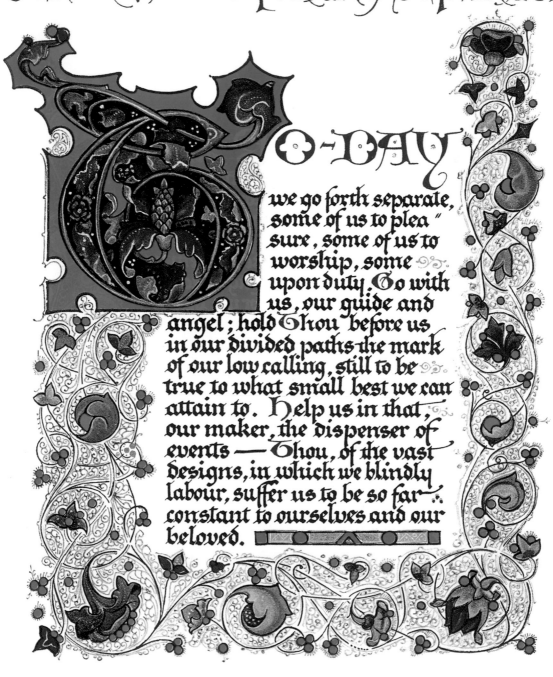

:BEFORE·A·TEMPORARY·SEPARATION·

TO-DAY we go forth separate, some of us to plea" sure, some of us to worship, some upon duty. Go with us, our guide and angel; hold Thou before us in our divided paths the mark of our low calling, still to be true to what small best we can attain to. Help us in that, our maker, the dispenser of events — Thou, of the vast designs, in which we blindly labour, suffer us to be so far constant to ourselves and our beloved.

·FOR·FRIENDS·

FOR our absent loved ones we implore thy loving-kindness. Keep them in life, keep them in growing honour; and for us, grant that we remain worthy of their love. For Christ's sake, let not our beloved blush for us, nor we for them. Grant us but that, and grant us courage to endure lesser ills unshaken, and to accept death, loss, and disappointment as it were straws upon the tide of life.

FOR·THE·FAMILY·

AID us, if it be thy
will, in our
concerns. Have mercy
on this land and innocent
people. Help them who
this day contend in dis-
appointment with their frailties.
Bless our family, bless our forest
house, bless our island helpers. Thou
who hast made for us this place of
ease and hope, accept and inflame
our gratitude; help us to repay, in
service one to another, the debt of
thine unmerited benefits and mer-
cies, so that, when the period of our
stewardship draws to a conclusion,
when the windows begin to be dark-
ened, when the bond of the family is
to be loosed, there shall be no bitter-
ness of remorse in our farewells.

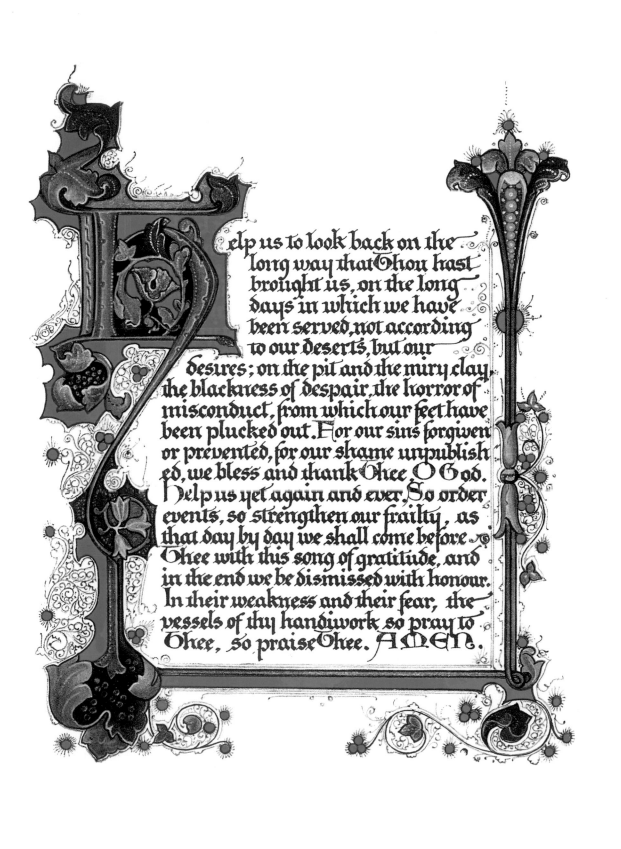

elp us to look back on the long way that Thou hast brought us, on the long days in which we have been served, not according to our deserts, but our desires: on the pit and the miry clay, the blackness of despair, the horror of misconduct, from which our feet have been plucked out. For our sins forgiven or prevented, for our shame unpublished, we bless and thank Thee O God. Help us yet again and ever. So order events, so strengthen our frailty, as that day by day we shall come before Thee with this song of gratitude, and in the end we be dismissed with honour. In their weakness and their fear, the vessels of thy handiwork so pray to Thee, so praise Thee. AMEN.

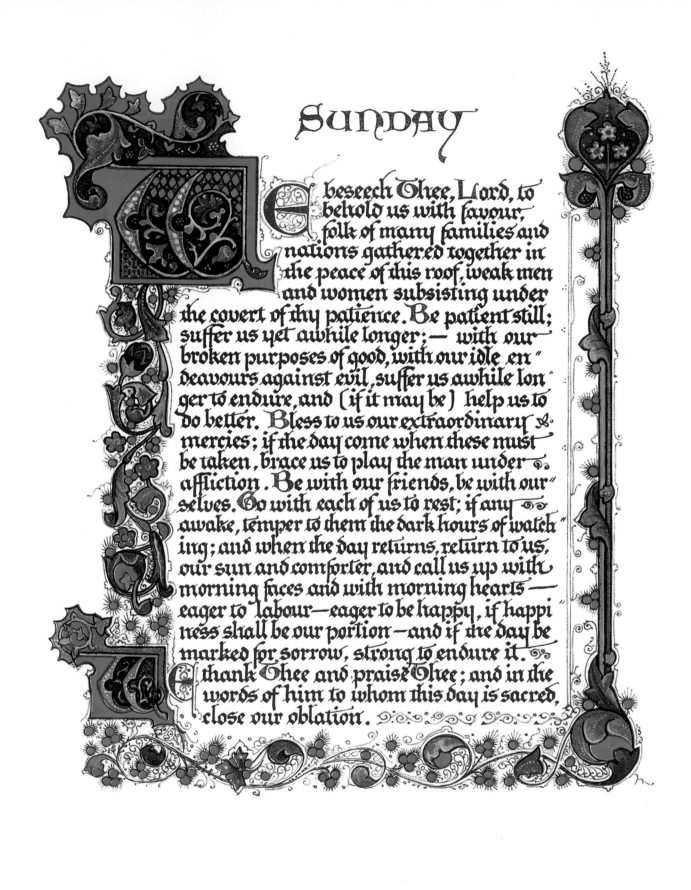

SUNDAY

WE beseech Thee, Lord, to behold us with favour, folk of many families and nations gathered together in the peace of this roof, weak men and women subsisting under the covert of thy patience. Be patient still; suffer us yet awhile longer;— with our broken purposes of good, with our idle endeavours against evil, suffer us awhile longer to endure, and (if it may be) help us to do better. Bless to us our extraordinary mercies; if the day come when these must be taken, brace us to play the man under affliction. Be with our friends, be with ourselves. Go with each of us to rest; if any awake, temper to them the dark hours of watching; and when the day returns, return to us, our sun and comforter, and call us up with morning faces and with morning hearts — eager to labour—eager to be happy, if happiness shall be our portion—and if the day be marked for sorrow, strong to endure it. We thank Thee and praise Thee; and in the words of him to whom this day is sacred, close our oblation.

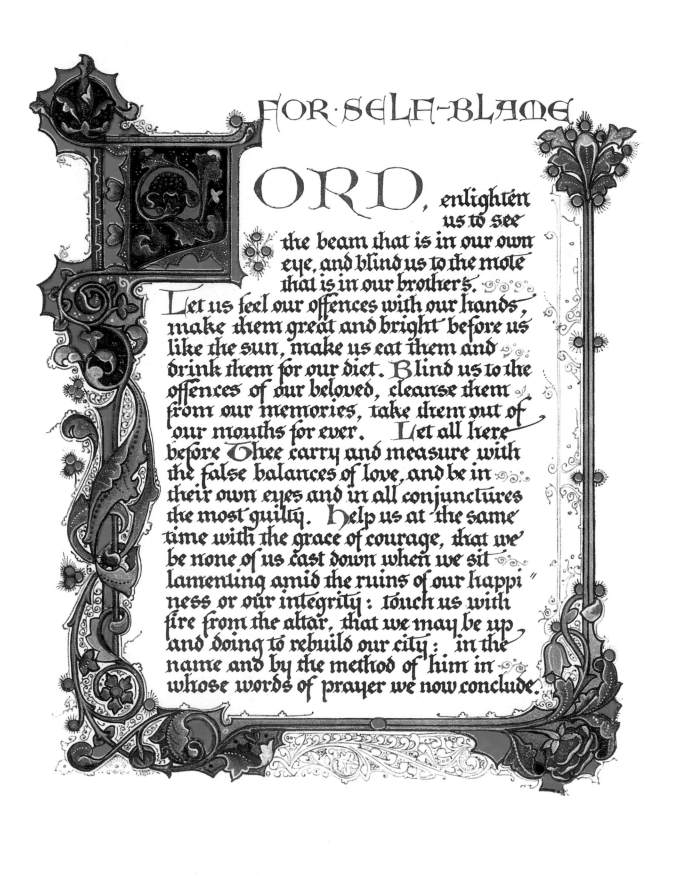

FOR·SELF-BLAME

LORD, enlighten us to see the beam that is in our own eye, and blind us to the mote that is in our brother's. Let us feel our offences with our hands, make them great and bright before us like the sun, make us eat them and drink them for our diet. Blind us to the offences of our beloved, cleanse them from our memories, take them out of our mouths for ever. Let all here before Thee carry and measure with the false balances of love, and be in their own eyes and in all conjunctures the most guilty. Help us at the same time with the grace of courage, that we be none of us cast down when we sit lamenting amid the ruins of our happiness or our integrity: touch us with fire from the altar, that we may be up and doing to rebuild our city: in the name and by the method of him in whose words of prayer we now conclude.

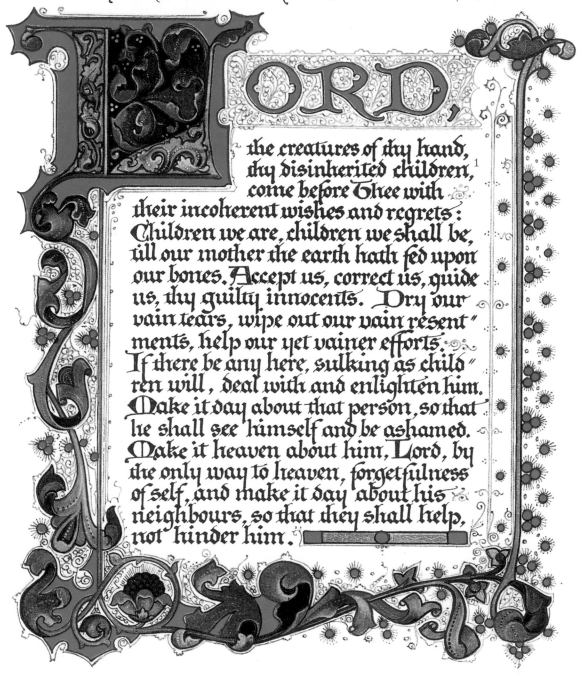

LORD,
the creatures of thy hand,
thy disinherited children,
come before Thee with [1]
their incoherent wishes and regrets:
Children we are, children we shall be,
till our mother the earth hath fed upon
our bones. Accept us, correct us, guide
us, thy guilty innocents. Dry our
vain tears, wipe out our vain resent-
ments, help our yet vainer efforts.
If there be any here, sulking as child-
ren will, deal with and enlighten him.
Make it day about that person, so that
he shall see himself and be ashamed.
Make it heaven about him, Lord, by
the only way to heaven, forgetfulness
of self, and make it day about his
neighbours, so that they shall help,
not hinder him.

E ARE
EVIL,
O GOD
and help us to
see it and amend.
We are good, and help us to
be better. Look down upon
thy servants with a patient
eye, even as Thou sendest
sun and rain; look down, call
upon the dry bones, quicken,
enliven; recreate in us the soul
of service, the spirit of peace;
renew in us the sense of joy.

Here end the Prayers of
Robert Louis Stevenson
as designed, written out
and illuminated by
Alberto Sangorski; reproduced
by the Graphic Engraving Co.
for Messrs Chatto & Windus,
who publish the volume at
111 St. Martin's Lane
London.   · MCMX ·

Notes
1 *Disinherited children:* We have disinherited ourselves like the prodigal son.
2 *We are good:* We are not good by nature; we are evil by nature. We are made good by God's grace.